Best Practices in Action

**SCHOLASTIC**

# Fluency Practice Mini-Books

## GRADE 1

By Kathleen M. Hollenbeck

NEW YORK • TORONTO • LONDON • AUCKLAND • SYDNEY
MEXICO CITY • NEW DELHI • HONG KONG • BUENOS AIRES

**Teaching** *Resources*

*To the patient*

*and dedicated teachers*

*who guide*

*and encourage students.*

Cover design by Maria Lilja
Interior design by Kathy Massaro
Interior art by Bari Weissman, Nadine Bernard Wescott, and Jenny Williams

ISBN: 0-439-55416-0
Copyright © 2005 by Kathleen M. Hollenbeck.
Published by Scholastic Inc.

3 4 5 6 7 8 9 10    40    13 12 11 10 09 08 07

# Contents

Introduction .......................................................................................... 4

**Fluency: An Overview** ......................................................................... 5

    What Is Fluency? .............................................................................. 5

    How Does Fluency Develop? ............................................................. 5

    Ways to Build Fluency ...................................................................... 6

    Bringing Oral Reading Into Your Classroom ...................................... 7

    Where Does Vocabulary Fit In? ......................................................... 8

    Enhancing Comprehension ................................................................ 8

**Assessing Fluency** .............................................................................. 9

    Teacher Checklist and Rubric for Oral Reading Fluency .................... 10

    Student Checklist for Self-Assessment ............................................. 11

**Using the Mini-Books to Enhance Fluency** ........................................ 12

    A Fluency Mini-Lesson ..................................................................... 12

    Mini-Book Readability Scores .......................................................... 14

    Preparing for Difficult or Unfamiliar Text ........................................ 15

    Activities for Building Fluency ......................................................... 16

    How to Make the Mini-Books ......................................................... 18

**Resources for Reading Fluency and Comprehension** ......................... 19

**The Mini-Books** ................................................................................ 21

    Cat Count ........................................................................................ 21

    I Am a Leaf! .................................................................................... 25

    How Do We Get to School? ............................................................. 29

    The Fly ............................................................................................ 33

    When Will My Seed Grow? .............................................................. 37

    What Do I See in the Dark? ............................................................ 41

    Where Did It Go? ............................................................................ 45

    No Pigs! ........................................................................................... 49

    Goldilocks Comes Back .................................................................... 53

    One Big Rock .................................................................................. 57

    The Sounds I Hear .......................................................................... 61

    What Do the Animals Do in Winter? ............................................... 65

    Helen Keller .................................................................................... 69

    Little Frog ....................................................................................... 73

    How the Bear Lost Its Tail ............................................................... 77

# INTRODUCTION

As educators, we believe there is power inherent in the written word. It is the power of knowledge and interaction—the ability to convey what we mean and to be heard, the gift that brings others' thoughts into our realm of understanding. It is our hope that the children in our care will learn to look to the written word for the same reasons we do—to answer questions, clarify learning, and exchange ideas.

A relationship between readers and the text can come only from training and experience. To help unlock the meaning of language, we teach readers to apply sense to symbols. They learn to associate sounds with letters and then to combine letters to make words. Ultimately, they connect these words to make sense of what they are reading. They can answer questions such as "What is this story about?" and "What is the author telling me?"

For some, this progression happens naturally. One day children are decoding single words and the next they are reading sentences, paragraphs, and chapters with ease. For others, each step comes with great effort, and success is not always at hand. They seek what the proficient readers have—and what all readers deserve: fluency.

Fluency, the ability to read with speed, accuracy, and expression, is essential to comprehension, which is the primary goal of reading. Fluency comes with practice, and all readers must strive to achieve it. Readers who are already fluent, readers who are well on their way to being so, and those who are struggling to get there all must employ practice and patience to become confident, capable readers. Their skills may be different, but their goal is the same: They want to understand.

This teaching resource, *Fluency Practice Mini-Books: Grade 1*, offers countless opportunities to build and strengthen your students' ability to read with ease and confidence. It contains 15 mini-books on topics from core curricular areas, tied in with national standards at the first-grade level and presented as fiction, nonfiction, poetry, and prose. It also offers tools for assessment, including a teacher checklist and rubric and a checklist students can use to monitor their own reading progress. (See Assessing Fluency, page 9.)

The mini-books and accompanying activities target specific skills in fluency and phonics and aim to increase speed of word recognition as well as to improve decoding accuracy, use of expression, and, ultimately, comprehension. The text adheres to vocabulary standards based on the studies of Harris and Jacobson. These standards ensure that your students will encounter words within the first-grade reading vocabulary rather than those that might hinder their progress.

The stories have been leveled using readability scores from the Lexile Framework for Reading (See chart, page 14.) These scores offer guidelines to help you select the stories that best match the needs and reading levels of each student. The stories are ready for use to practice, strengthen, and assess skills in reading fluency. And they all share the same objective: to give students practice reading comfortably, confidently, and with enthusiasm, so that you can build an ever-growing flock of fluent readers within the walls of your classroom.

# Fluency: An Overview

## What Is Fluency?

Fluency is the mark of a proficient reader. When a student reads text quickly, gets most of the words right, and uses appropriate expression and phrasing, we say that he or she has achieved fluency. Fluency frees readers from the struggle that slows them down. Hence, they are able to read for meaning and to understand. They can attend to the details of text, pausing as indicated and varying tone and pace to enhance comprehension for both themselves and potential listeners.

## How Does Fluency Develop?

As with every skill worth developing, fluency sharpens with experience. Exposure to print, immersion in a rich linguistic environment, and practice, practice, practice all lead to fluent reading.

From the emergent on up, readers must learn and apply tools to help them advance. The National Institute for Literacy (NIFL) speaks of fluency as a skill in flux.

> "Fluency is not a stage of development at which readers can read all words quickly and easily. Fluency changes, depending on what readers are reading, their familiarity with the words, and the amount of their practice with reading text. Even very skilled readers may read in a slow, labored manner when reading texts with many unfamiliar words or topics." (NIFL, 2001)

Readers are most comfortable (and most fluent) when reading what they have seen before or what they know most about. When venturing beyond that, they must rely on word attack skills, prior knowledge, and the host of tools that helped them advance previously.

> "Fluent readers read aloud effortlessly and with expression. Their reading sounds natural, as if they are speaking. Readers who have not yet developed fluency read slowly, word by word. Their oral reading is choppy and plodding."
>
> NATIONAL INSTITUTE FOR LITERACY, 2001

# Ways to Build Fluency

Two words encompass what readers require for the development of fluency: *exposure* and *practice*. To foster fluent reading, be sure to:

✳ **MODEL FLUENT READING.** Read aloud to students. As you read, model (and point out) aspects of fluent reading such as phrasing, pacing, and expression. Help students understand that people aren't born knowing how to do this; they learn it by hearing it and trying it themselves.

✳ **PROVIDE STUDENTS WITH PLENTY OF READING PRACTICE.** Oral reading is highly effective for tracking and strengthening fluency. It enables both the reader and the listener to hear the reader and assess progress, and it allows the listener to provide guidance as needed. Whisper reading serves as a transition from oral to silent reading. In whisper reading, all students read aloud at the same time, but at a volume that is just barely audible. The student is able to self-monitor and the teacher to move around the room, noting progress, keeping students on task, and offering guidance as needed. For silent reading, students read an assigned passage or a book of their own choice. Because the reader cannot be heard, assessment of reading skill is not possible. The value of silent reading is that it increases time spent reading and gives students "opportunities to expand and practice reading strategies." (Fountas and Pinnell, 2001)

✳ **SELECT APPROPRIATE TEXT.** To develop fluency, a student must practice reading text at his or her independent reading level—the level at which he or she is able to accurately decode 96 to 100 percent of the words in a given text. This level varies for every student. By assessing each student's reading level up front, you will be prepared to select appropriate texts and ensure that your students get a lot of practice reading at a level at which they achieve success. (Rasinski, 2003; Worthy and Broaddus, 2001/2002) For information about how to use text to assess fluency, see Assessing Fluency, page 9.

✳ **RAISE THE BAR.** Read aloud to students from text that is above their independent reading level, exposing them to new and more difficult words and concepts without the pressure of having to decode.

✳ **GIVE ROOM TO GROW.** To help a student advance in fluency, present text at his or her instructional level. This text can be read with 90 to 95 percent accuracy. With a little help, the student can get almost all the words right. (Blevins, 2001a; Rasinski, 2003)

✳ **PROVIDE DIRECT INSTRUCTION AND FEEDBACK.** Prepare students before they read. First, review phonics skills they will need to decode words. Draw attention to sight words, root words, affixes, and word chunks. Pre-teach difficult or unfamiliar words. Demonstrate the use of intonation, phrasing, and expression, and tell children when they have done these well. Listen to children read, and offer praise as well as helpful tips for the next attempt.

> "Fluency develops when children do lots of reading and writing—including lots of easy text. Repeated reading helps children develop fluency because with each reading their word identification becomes quicker and more automatic, freeing attention for expression, phrasing, and comprehension."
>
> (CUNNINGHAM, 2005)

* **USE A VARIETY OF READING MATERIALS.** Plays, fiction stories, nonfiction passages, and poetry offer a rich and varied reading experience. Expose your students to each of these. Give them many opportunities to get excited about and immerse themselves in what they are reading.

* **HIGHLIGHT PHRASING.** One of the most effective ways to help students who are struggling with fluency is to use phrase-cued text. Phrase-cued text is marked by slashes to indicate where readers should pause. One slash indicates a pause or a meaningful chunk of text within a sentence. Two slashes indicate a longer pause at the end of a sentence. Ready-made samples of phrase-cued text are available (see Resources for Reading Fluency and Comprehension, page 19), but you can also convert any passage of text to phrase-cued text by reading it aloud, listening for pauses and meaningful chunks of text, and drawing slashes in the appropriate places. (See the example, right, from the mini-book "Little Frog," page 73.) Model fluent reading with proper phrasing, and invite students to practice with the text you have marked.

> ### Little Frog
>
> Little Frog/ didn't like/ his color.//
> "I don't want/ to be green,"/ he said.//
>
> Little Frog/ hopped into/ a can of paint.//
> He hopped/ out again.// The paint/ was red.//
> Now Little Frog/ was red,/ too.//
>
> Little Frog/ hopped/ down the road.//
> A cat/ saw him/ go by.//
> "A red bird!"/ said the cat.// "I'll eat it!"//
> "I'm not a bird!"/ cried Little Frog.//

> "Students who are having trouble with comprehension may not be putting words together in meaningful phrases or chunks as they read. Their oral reading is characterized by a choppy, word-by-word delivery that impedes comprehension. These students need instruction in phrasing written text into appropriate segments."
>
> (BLEVINS, 2001A)

## Bringing Oral Reading Into Your Classroom

Provide opportunities for children to read aloud. This may include all or any of the following:

* **INTERACTIVE READ-ALOUD:** An adult reader demonstrates fluent oral reading and talks about how he or she changes tone, pace, or expression in response to the story. Students enjoy a dramatic reading and absorb skills in fluent reading. In addition, the interactive read-aloud provides an opportunity for teachers to ask open-ended questions before, during, and after the reading, soliciting students' prior knowledge and extending their understanding, comprehension, and connection with the topic. This connection can advance student interaction with the text and promote optimal conditions for fluency.

* **SHARED READING:** An adult reader models fluent reading and then invites children to read along, using big books or small-group instruction.

> As the child approaches a new text he is entitled to an introduction so that when he reads, the gist of the whole or partly revealed story can provide some guide for a fluent reading. He will understand what he reads if it refers to things he knows about, or has read about previously, so that he is familiar with the topic, the vocabulary or the story itself.
>
> (CLAY, 1991)

✳ **CHORAL READING:** An adult and children read aloud together. This activity works especially well with poetry and cumulative tales.

✳ **ECHO READING:** A child repeats phrases or sentences read by someone else, mimicking tone, expression, and pacing.

✳ **REPEATED READING:** An adult reads aloud while a student listens and reads again while the student follows along. Then the adult invites the student to read along, and, finally, the student reads the same text aloud alone. This technique is most helpful for struggling readers.

✳ **PAIRED REPEATED READING:** Teachers group students in pairs, matching above-level readers with on-level readers and on-level readers with those below level. Partners are encouraged to take turns reading aloud to each other, each reading a short passage three times and then getting feedback. The manner of grouping provides every struggling reader with a more proficient reader to model.

✳ **READERS' THEATER:** Students work in groups to rehearse and perform a brief play before the class. Performing can be exciting, and the drive to present well can be a powerful force behind mastering fluency in reading and speech, motivating both struggling and proficient readers.

✳ **TAPE-ASSISTED READING:** Children listen to books-on-tape while reading along in a book. (Consider recording your own tapes if commercially made tapes go too quickly, or if the tapes include background elements such as music or sound effects, which can be distracting.) Children can also listen and critique their own reading on tape.

✳ **PHRASE-CUED TEXT:** (See Highlight Phrasing, page 7.)

## Where Does Vocabulary Fit In?

Stumbling over the words constitutes one of the main setbacks on the way to fluency. It remains in your students' best interest, then, to grow familiar with words they will likely encounter in reading. Cunningham and Allington (2003) urge active use of word walls, inviting student participation in choosing words to put on the walls, eliminating words hardly used, and reviewing the list words daily.

## Enhancing Comprehension

In all reading instruction, it is important to remember that reading imparts meaning, and so the fundamental goal of reading is to comprehend. All other instruction—phonics, phonemic awareness, auditory discrimination—is wasted effort if comprehension gets lost in the process. Consequently, those who find no purpose or meaning in the written word will soon lose interest in reading altogether.

Avoid this by teaching your students strategies to enhance comprehension. Help them learn to question the text they are reading. *What is the message?*

*Does it make sense to them? Do they know what it means?* Find out by asking questions. Ask questions before students read, to prepare them for the story. Ask as they read, to deepen their understanding of the text. Ask additional questions after they read, to clear up any comprehension issues and summarize the story. Teach your students to formulate questions of their own to give them a vested interest in what they are reading.

# Assessing Fluency

There are two ways to assess a student's progress in fluency: informally and formally. Informal assessment involves listening to students read aloud, noting how easily, quickly, and accurately they read and deciding how well they attend to phrasing, expression, and other elements. Formal assessment involves timing a student's oral reading to create a tangible record of his or her progress throughout the school year.

To conduct an informal assessment of students' reading fluency, use the reproducible Teacher Checklist and Rubric for Oral Reading Fluency, on page 10. Have a student read aloud for five to seven minutes while you note on the form the strategies the student uses as well as his or her reading strengths and difficulties.

Students can monitor their own progress using the Student Checklist for Self-Assessment, on page 11. Photocopy and laminate one for each student. Review the checklist components with students many times, until they understand the purpose of the checklist and the meaning of each sentence. Encourage students to mentally complete the checklist from time to time to track their own reading fluency.

To carry out timed repeated reading, select a passage of text (150–250 words) that is at the student's independent reading level and that he or she has never read before. Have the student read aloud the passage for one minute. Track your own copy of the text while he or she reads, marking words omitted or pronounced incorrectly. Count the number of words the student read correctly. Then give the student three one-minute opportunities (in separate sessions) to read the same text, and average the scores to obtain his or her oral reading fluency rate.*

## In Conclusion

Does fluency instruction work? Research has shown that concentrated reading instruction can dramatically improve reading comprehension and fluency, which in turn affect academic performance, self-esteem, and overall achievement. With this in mind, it is not only helpful to instruct with an eye toward fluency, it is essential.

---

* For more detailed information on timed reading, consult Blevins (2001a, pp. 9–12) and Rasinski (2003, pp. 82–83).

> "Instruction that focuses too heavily on word-perfect decoding sends a message that good reading is nothing more than accurate word recognition. As a result, students tend to shoot for accuracy at the expense of everything else, including meaning."
>
> (RASINSKI, 2004)

> "The majority of children who enter kindergarten and elementary school at risk for reading failure can learn to read at average or above-average levels—if they are identified early and given systematic, intensive instruction in phonemic awareness, phonics, reading fluency, vocabulary, and reading comprehension strategies."
>
> (LYON AND CHHABRA, 2004; ORIGINALLY CREDITED TO LYON ET AL., 2001 AND TORGESEN, 2002)

Child's Name: _____ Date: _____

Grade: _____ Passage: _____

# Teacher Checklist and Rubric for Oral Reading Fluency

## Oral Reading Checklist

| The reader: | Usually | Sometimes | Seldom |
|---|---|---|---|
| self-corrects as he or she reads. ............................................. | _____ | _____ | _____ |
| attempts to read/pronounce unfamiliar words. ............................. | _____ | _____ | _____ |
| reads in meaningful phrases or word chunks. .............................. | _____ | _____ | _____ |
| reads smoothly without frequent pauses. .................................... | _____ | _____ | _____ |
| attends to punctuation at the end of a sentence. ........................ | _____ | _____ | _____ |
| reads with appropriate expression. ............................................ | _____ | _____ | _____ |

## Oral Reading Rubric

**4** The child reads in meaningful phrases. The child responds to punctuation through appropriate pausing and intonation. The child usually self-corrects while reading. The child reads with expression and works to pronounce unfamiliar words, repeating them if necessary to ensure accuracy.

**3** The child reads primarily in meaningful phrases. The child attends to most punctuation and usually reads at a smooth pace, but sometimes struggles with words or sentence structure. The child often self-corrects but does not always recognize errors. The child reads with expression and attempts to pronounce unfamiliar words, but sometimes needs assistance.

**2** The child reads primarily in groups of two or three words. The child reads smoothly at times and then slowly, word by word, especially when encountering unfamiliar words. The child pays little attention to punctuation, pacing, and expression and spends most of the effort on decoding. The child hesitates before trying new words and usually requires assistance with them.

**1** The child reads slowly and word by word. The child does not heed punctuation and reads words in a string without pause or expression. The child does not attempt to pronounce unfamiliar words. The child's reading sounds stilted and unnatural and lacks meaning.

Adapted from *35 Rubrics & Checklists to Assess Reading and Writing* by Adele Fiderer. Scholastic, 1998. Permission to reuse granted by the author.

*Fluency Practice Mini-Books: Grade 1* Scholastic Teaching Resources

Name: _____

# My Read-Aloud Checklist

| | | Yes | Sometimes | No |
|---|---|---|---|---|
| **1** | I say a word again if it does not sound right. | ☐ | ☐ | ☐ |
| **2** | I pay attention to punctuation at the end of a sentence. | ☐ | ☐ | ☐ |
| **3** | I try to read without stopping after every word. | ☐ | ☐ | ☐ |
| **4** | I read with expression. | ☐ | ☐ | ☐ |
| **5** | I look at the pictures to see what is happening. | ☐ | ☐ | ☐ |

Adapted from *35 Rubrics & Checklists to Assess Reading and Writing* by Adele Fiderer.
Permission to reuse granted by the author.
*Fluency Practice Mini-Books: Grade 1*   Scholastic Teaching Resources

# Using the Mini-Books to Enhance Fluency

## A Fluency Mini-Lesson

Use this sample mini-lesson as a model for using the mini-books to strengthen and assess students' reading fluency.

### MINI-BOOK 1
### Cat Count

**PREPARATION:** Give each student a copy of the mini-book "Cat Count" (pages 21–24). Help students assemble the books, or construct them in advance. (See How to Make the Mini-Books, page 18.)

### Pre-Reading

**1.** Introduce unfamiliar or difficult words that students will come across in the text. These might include *row, loud,* and *good-bye* as well as some of the more complex sight words, such as *where, behind,* and *which*. Help students decode the words. Review them several times to aid recognition and boost fluency. (See Preparing for Difficult or Unfamiliar Text, page 15, for more about the vocabulary in the mini-books.)

**2.** Review reading techniques that promote fluency, such as reading from left to right, "smooshing" words together to sound like talking, and crossing the page with a steady, sweeping eye movement. (Blevins, 2001a)

### Reading and Modeling

**1.** Depending on students' level of reading proficiency, you may want to read aloud the story first and then invite them to read along with you in their mini-books. As you read, point out ways in which your pacing, intonation, and expression lend meaning to the text. You might say:

> "Did you notice how my voice rose at the end of the sentence 'Where does he go'? That's what we do when we see a question mark. We know the sentence is asking something; we use our voices to make it sound that way."

or

> "Listen while I reread the words, 'Good-bye! Good-bye!' What did I do with my voice to make those words sound cheerful? What did I see in the sentences that told me to do that?" (*exclamation points*)

I see ten cats,
ten in a row.
One runs away.
Where does he go?

①

I hear nine cats.
Nine loud cats cry.
Three look for food.
Good-bye! Good-bye!

②

Six cats at play.
They jump and run.
One takes a nap.
Five still have fun.

③

Five cats want food.
Some fish they find.
Two eat and run.
Three stay behind.

④

I see three cats.
They look at me.
My mom says "No."
I can't have three.

⑤

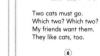

Two cats must go.
Which two? Which two?
My friends want them.
They like cats, too.

⑥

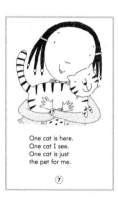

One cat is here.
One cat I see.
One cat is just
the pet for me.

⑦

**2.** Try reading the sentences without the inflection. Point out that questions read without the appropriate tone sound flat and stilted, without depth, character, or expression.

**3.** Read the story aloud again, inviting students to read aloud with you as they are able. NOTE: If you feel that a group of readers is already proficient, preview the words and then have children read the story aloud without modeling.

**4.** Once readers have read the story several times, go back and emphasize aspects of phonics and vocabulary that will increase their understanding of language; encourage faster, more accurate reading; and deepen comprehension. (You may want to write the story on sentence strips and use a pocket chart to manipulate words and phrases.) "Cat Count" presents opportunities to explore such topics as:

* **homonyms:** *two, too.* Have students put a dot under the homonyms in the book.

* **rhyming:** *row, go; run, fun; find, behind.* Have students underline the rhyming words in each verse.

* **number words:** *ten, nine, six, five, three, two, one.* Have students circle all the number words in the mini-book.

* **phrasing:** Readers must pause after all ending punctuation. They will pause for a shorter time between the two sentences that stand side-by-side and are meant to be read more quickly: "Which two? Which two?"

* **dialogue:** Help readers practice using clues in punctuation, text placement, and vocabulary to determine who is speaking and when. Point out that each time a character speaks, the words that he or she says are contained within quotation marks. An indented paragraph indicates that a new speaker is talking. Dialogue words such as "said" and "cried" highlight who is speaking.

**5.** The methods described here feature interactive read-aloud and shared reading. Other options for use with this mini-book include timed reading for assessment of each child's rate of fluency, paired repeated reading, and choral reading.

Fluency techniques such as Readers' Theater work well with stories that are rich in dialogue—for example, "One Big Rock," page 57, and "Little Frog," page 73. Echo reading works best with repetitive or rhythmic text, which naturally lead the reader to pause in the middle of a sentence rather than strictly at the end. This method gives students the opportunity to step in and participate in the oral reading. "I Am a Leaf!," page 25, and "The Sounds I Hear," page 61, offer examples of such text.

# Mini-Book Readability Scores

The chart below shows the readability scores of the stories in this collection. The texts were leveled using the Lexile Framework for Reading. These scores offer guidelines to help you select the stories that best match the needs and reading levels of each student. For more information about the Lexile Framework, go to www.lexile.com. (See Preparing for Difficult or Unfamiliar Text, page 15, for more about the vocabulary in the mini-books.)

| Story Title | Lexile Score |
|---|---|
| 1. Cat Count | BR |
| 2. I Am a Leaf! | BR |
| 3. How Do We Get to School? | 30L |
| 4. The Fly | 40L |
| 5. When Will My Seed Grow? | 50L |
| 6. What Do I See in the Dark? | 80L |
| 7. Where Did It Go? | 90L |
| 8. No Pigs! | 160L |
| 9. Goldilocks Comes Back | 170L |
| 10. One Big Rock | 190L |
| 11. The Sounds I Hear | 220L |
| 12. What Do the Animals Do in Winter? | 230L |
| 13. Helen Keller | 240L |
| 14. Little Frog | 250L |
| 15. How the Bear Lost Its Tail | 250L |

**BR** = Beginning Reader

**L** = Lexile score

Texts that score from BR to 250L are appropriate for students who are at the first-grade independent reading level.

# Preparing for Difficult or Unfamiliar Text

To assess fluency, have children read text that is new to them. (Blevins, 2001a) With this in mind, when using the mini-books for assessment, do not prepare students by introducing unfamiliar or difficult words. Pre-reading may distort the assessment results.

Before reading for the purpose of developing fluency, however, it is helpful to highlight words that may prove to be stumbling blocks for young or struggling readers. Words slightly above grade level, difficult words on grade level, and complex high-frequency words can be daunting when encountered for the first time within text. To prevent this, introduce words and help children decode them before they read. Give them a chance to decipher the words before you provide correct pronunciation. Then review the words several times to aid recognition and boost fluency.

The words listed below may be unfamiliar or challenging to your students. Some are within the common first grade vocabulary but may contain difficult or unfamiliar letter patterns. Others have been categorized as common to text read by slightly older readers. (Harris and Jacobson, 1982) These words were selected for use in the mini-books when necessary to enhance the flow of the text or where substitutions would not carry the same meaning, such as the words *frog* in "Little Frog," page 73, and *fur* in "What Do the Animals Do in Winter?," page 65. Note that proper nouns are excluded from leveling.

**Cat Count**
*row, loud, good-bye, friends*

**I Am a Leaf!**
*leaf, wind, blows, street, people, heavy, begun*

**How Do We Get to School?**
*school, street, full, family, trucks, outside, matter*

**The Fly**
*flew, anything, bathroom, teddy, lunch, cried, shut, inside*

**When Will My Seed Grow?**
*dig, seed, earth, something, leaves, bud, flower*

**What Do I See in the Dark?**
*tall, horse, small, chair, dresser, course*

**Where Did It Go?**
*school, wind, hung, leaf, pond, stoplight, landed, high, kite, laughed*

**No Pigs!**
*wolf, full, cried, none*

**Goldilocks Comes Back**
*Goldilocks, sorry, breaking, chair, pictures, wall*

**One Big Rock**
*rock, pick, tall, lifted, strong, bugs*

**The Sounds I Hear**
*streets, cream, family*

**What Do the Animals Do in Winter?**
*winter, leaves, warmer, close, fur, frogs, ground, happens, spring*

**Helen Keller**
*Helen Keller, alone, Anne, school, loud*

**Little Frog**
*frog, paint, mud, worm, pond*

**How the Bear Lost Its Tail**
*laughed, tail, felt, tried, cried*

# Activities for Building Fluency

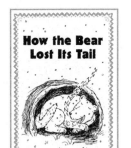

## ● Attend to Punctuation

Emphasize the impact of ending punctuation. Model and then invite students to say the same sentence three different ways, using a period, a question mark, and an exclamation point. For example, from "How the Bear Lost Its Tail," page 77, you might read the sentence "He jumped at the fox" as follows:

* ✳ "He jumped at the fox."

* ✳ "He jumped at the fox?"

* ✳ "He jumped at the fox!"

## ● Explore Dialogue

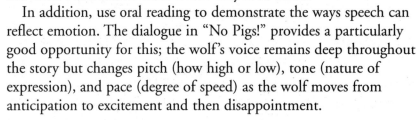

Use a mini-book filled with conversation, such as "One Big Rock," page 57, or "No Pigs!," page 49, to draw attention to using dialogue to represent each character's unique personality. For example, when reading aloud "One Big Rock," purposely model distinct voices for Joe, Ted, Ben, and Kim. Discuss the ways you change inflection, accent, pace, and tone to represent each character. When Ted speaks, for example, you may want to talk slowly and carefully. For Kim, you may choose to speak more quickly and in a higher-pitched voice. Each character's speech will hold its own distinct sound; repeat it each time he or she speaks. Point out your intentions to your students, and encourage them to create their own unique voices for characters—in this mini-book and in trade books they read aloud.

In addition, use oral reading to demonstrate the ways speech can reflect emotion. The dialogue in "No Pigs!" provides a particularly good opportunity for this; the wolf's voice remains deep throughout the story but changes pitch (how high or low), tone (nature of expression), and pace (degree of speed) as the wolf moves from anticipation to excitement and then disappointment.

## Connect With Phonics

Each mini-book offers opportunities to extend phonics awareness. While reading, look for connections to the following:

### Letter-Sound Relationships

✳ blends and digraphs

✳ high-frequency words

✳ vowel sounds

✳ word families

✳ rhyme

### Word Structure

✳ compound words

✳ contractions

✳ homonyms

✳ plurals

✳ prefixes and suffixes

✳ syllabication

Helen Keller

## Identify Key Text Features With Highlighting Tape

Use colorful highlighting tape to flag words previously introduced as well as to mark the beginning and end of text children will be expected to read. Students can also use highlighting tape to emphasize punctuation, repetitive phrases, rhyming words, sight words, and word chunks, as well as to mark dialogue for Readers' Theater.

Little Frog

## Reinforce Understanding With a Pocket Chart

Use a pocket chart to reinforce pacing, intonation, chunking, and other aspects of fluent reading. Focus on one mini-book and one skill at a time. For example, to guide children in reading a sentence smoothly instead of word by word, determine where natural phrasing groups words together, such as "Some animals sleep" in the sentence "Some animals sleep all winter" (from the mini-book "What Do the Animals Do in Winter?," page 65). Write each word on its own strip, and place these words in order on the chart. Read the words aloud, separately at first, and then blending, or "smooshing," them together. (Blevins, 2001a) Next, substitute the individual words for a larger strip featuring the words in a group rather than individually. (Example: "Some animals sleep" would be a natural word group.)

Invite children to manipulate sentences on the pocket chart, writing whole sentences on strips and then cutting them apart to show natural groupings.

# How to Make the Mini-Books

**1.** Remove the mini-book pages to be copied, tearing along the perforation.

**2.** For each book, make a double-sided copy of the pages on 8 1/2- by 11-inch copy paper.

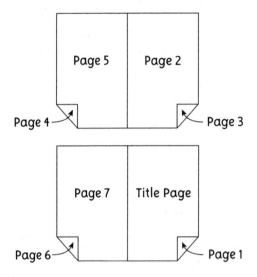

**3.** Once you have double-sided copies of the pages, place page 2 behind the title page.

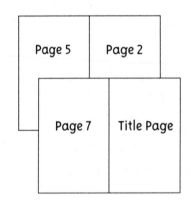

**4.** Fold the pages in half along the solid line.

**5.** Check to be sure that the pages are in proper order, and then staple them together along the book's spine.

# Resources for Reading Fluency and Comprehension

Armbruster, Bonnie B., Ph.D., Fran Lehr, M.A., and Jean Osborn, M.Ed., *A Child Becomes a Reader.* (RMC Research Corporation/Partnership for Reading: National Institute for Literacy, National Institute of Child Health and Human Development, U.S. Department of Education, and U.S. Department of Health and Human Services, 2003).

Beck, Isabel L., Margaret G. McKeown, and Linda Kucan. *Bringing Words to Life: Robust Vocabulary Instruction.* New York: The Guilford Press, 2002.

Blevins, Wiley. *Building Fluency: Lessons and Strategies for Reading Success.* New York: Scholastic, 2001a.*

Blevins, Wiley. *Teaching Phonics and Word Study.* New York: Scholastic, 2001b.

Clay, Marie M. *Becoming Literate: The Construction of Inner Control.* Portsmouth, NH: Heinemann, 1991.

Cunningham, Patricia M., *Phonics They Use: Words for Reading and Writing.* Boston: Pearson Education, Inc., 2005.

Cunningham, Patricia M., and Richard L. Allington. *Classrooms That Work: They Can ALL Read and Write.* New York: Pearson Education, 2003.

Cunningham, Patricia M., Dorothy P. Hall, and Cheryl M. Sigmon. *The Teacher's Guide to the Four Blocks.* Greensboro, NC: Carson-Dellosa, 1999.

Fiderer, Adele. *40 Rubrics & Checklists to Assess Reading and Writing.* New York: Scholastic, 1999.

Fiderer, Adele. *35 Rubrics & Checklists to Assess Reading and Writing.* New York: Scholastic, 1998.

*Fluency Formula: Grades 1–6.* New York: Scholastic, 2003.*

Fountas, Irene C., and Gay Su Pinnell. *Guiding Readers and Writers (Grades 3–6): Teaching Comprehension, Genre, and Content Literacy.* Portsmouth, NH: Heinemann, 2001.

Fresch, Mary Jo, and Aileen Wheaton. *Teaching and Assessing Spelling.* New York: Scholastic, 2002.

Harris, A. J., and M. D. Jacobson. *Basic Reading Vocabularies.* New York: Macmillan, 1982.

Heilman, Arthur W. *Phonics in Perspective.* Upper Saddle River, NJ: Pearson Education, 2002.

Kieff, Judith. "Revisiting the Read-Aloud." *Childhood Education*. Volume 80, No. 1, p. 28.

Lyon, G. R., J. M. Fletcher, S. E. Shaywitz, B. A. Shaywitz, J. K. Torgesen, F. B. Wood, A. Shulte, and R. Olson. "Rethinking Learning Disabilities." In C. E. Finn, R. A. J. Rotherham, and C. R. Hokanson (Eds.), *Rethinking Special Education for a New Century*. Washington, D.C.: Thomas B. Fordham Foundation & Progressive Policy Institute, 2001, pp. 259–287.

Lyon, G. Reid. "Why Reading Is Not a Natural Process." *Educational Leadership*, Volume 55, No. 6 (March 1998): pp. 14–18.

Lyon, G. Reid, and Vinita Chhabra. "The Science of Reading Research." *Educational Leadership*, Volume 61, No. 6 (March 2004): pp. 12–17.

Pennington, Mark. *Better Spelling in 5 Minutes a Day*. Roseville, CA: Prima Publishing, 2001.

Pinnell, Gay Su, and Patricia L. Scharer. *Teaching for Comprehension in Reading*. New York: Scholastic, 2003.*

Rasinski, Timothy. "Creating Fluent Readers." *Educational Leadership*, Volume 61, No. 6 (March 2004): pp. 46–51.

Rasinski, Timothy V. *The Fluent Reader*. New York: Scholastic, 2003.*

Tomlinson, Carol Ann. *The Differentiated Classroom*. Alexandria, VA: ASCD, 1999.

Torgesen, J. K. "The Prevention of Reading Difficulties." *Journal of School Psychology*, Volume 40, Issue 1, pp. 7–26.

Wagstaff, Janiel M. *Teaching Reading and Writing With Word Walls*. New York: Scholastic, 1999.

White, Sheida. "Listening to Children Read Aloud: Oral Fluency." *NAEP Facts*, National Center for Education Statistics. Volume 1, Number 1.

Worthy, Jo, and Karen Broaddus. "Fluency Beyond the Primary Grades: From Group Performance to Silent, Independent Reading." *The Reading Teacher*, Volume 55, No. 4, (December 2001/January 2002): pp. 334–343.

Worthy, Jo, and Kathryn Prater. "I Thought About It All Night: Readers Theatre for Reading Fluency and Motivation (The Intermediate Grades)." *The Reading Teacher*, Volume 56, No. 3 (November 2002): p. 294.

Yopp, Hallie Kay, and Ruth Helen Yopp. "Supporting Phonemic Awareness Development in the Classroom." *The Reading Teacher*, Volume 54, No. 2 (October 2000): pp. 130–143.

---

* This resource includes samples and/or examples of phrase-cued text.

# Cat Count

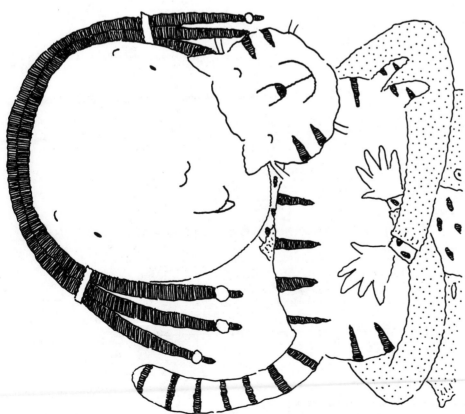

One cat is here.
One cat I see.
One cat is just
the pet for me.

⑦

I see ten cats,
ten in a row.
One runs away.
Where does he go?

1

Two cats must go.
Which two? Which two?
My friends want them.
They like cats, too.

6

I hear nine cats.
Nine loud cats cry.
Three look for food.
Good-bye! Good-bye!

②

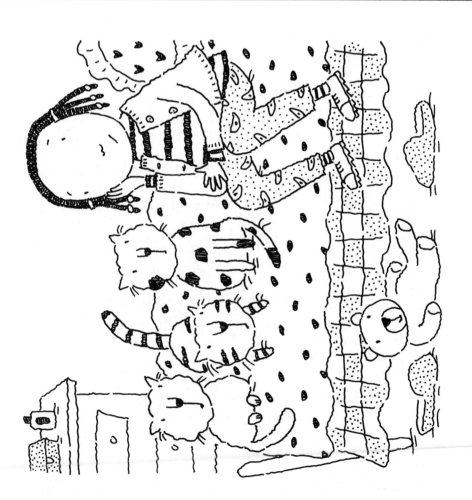

I see three cats.
They look at me.
My mom says "No."
I can't have three.

⑤

Six cats at play.
They jump and run.
One takes a nap.
Five still have fun.

③

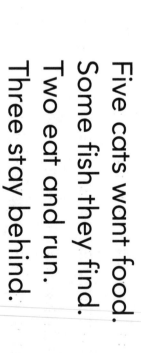

Five cats want food.
Some fish they find.
Two eat and run.
Three stay behind.

④

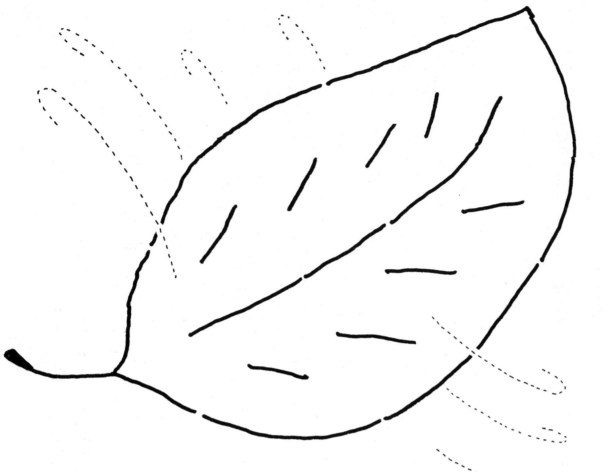

# I Am a Leaf!

I am a leaf!
I'm light and I'm small.
Yellow and red,
the colors of fall.

⑦

I am a leaf!
I fall from the tree.
Down, down I go.
The grass catches me.

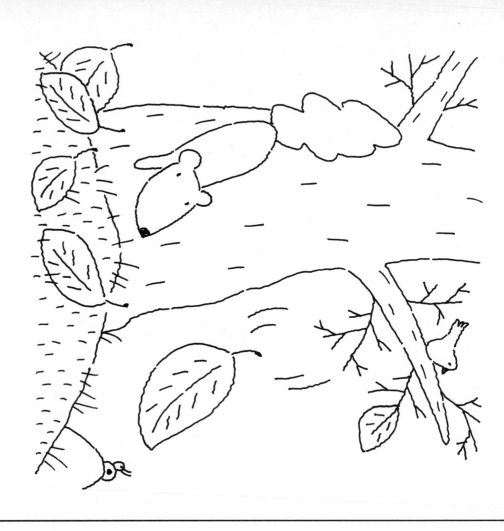

1

I am a leaf!
Now day has begun.
Heat comes, and light!
I dry in the sun.

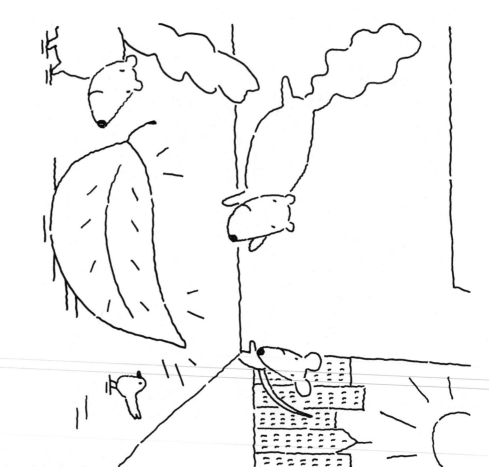

6

I am a leaf!
How hard the wind blows!
It picks me up.
I go where it goes.

②

I am a leaf!
The rain falls all night.
Wind can't move me.
I'm heavy, not light.

⑤

I am a leaf!
I race down the street.
People walk by.
I'm right at their feet.

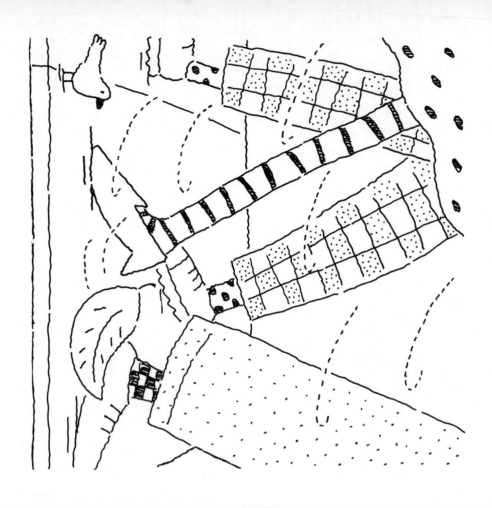

③

I am a leaf!
I feel the rain fall.
Now I am wet.
I can't move at all.

④

# How Do We Get to School?

Walk or ride?
What do you say?
How did you get
to school today?

⑦

How do we get to school
each day?
We walk or ride.
We go our way!

(1)

It does not matter
how we go.
We all must get
to school, we know.

(6)

We walk to school.
It's on our street.
We walk there on
our own two feet.

②

We ride to school.
On bikes we ride.
We go right in.
Bikes stay outside.

⑤

We ride to school.
We take a bus.
It's full.
There are a lot of us.

We ride to school
with family.
We ride in cars
and trucks, you see.

# The Fly

I found him where it all began.
I opened up the door.
At last, the little fly flew out.
But in came seven more!

7

A fly came in with me today.
I could not get him out.
He would not let me near him.
How fast he flew about!

I found him in my lunch box.
"I'll get you now!" I cried.
I shut the top. I opened it.
The fly was not inside.

I found him on a window.
"I'll let him out!" I said.
Before I could do anything,
that fly went by my head.

②

I found him on a pile of things.
He hid under a shoe.
He did not stay there very long.
I moved. Away he flew.

⑤

I found him in the bathroom.
He walked right up the wall.
He must have seen me coming.
He headed down the hall.

③

I found him on my teddy bear.
He stayed there. He was still.
I jumped at him. He got away.
"I'll get you! Yes, I will!"

④

# When Will My Seed Grow?

The bud opens.
What I see is pink.
My seed has done its work.
It is a flower!

(7)

I dig a hole.
I put in a seed.
I pat the earth on top.
When will my seed grow?

1

The green grows tall.
I see two small leaves.
A bud grows at the top.
Look at my seed grow!

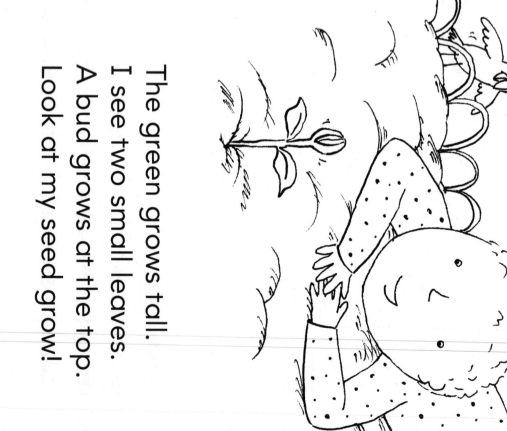

6

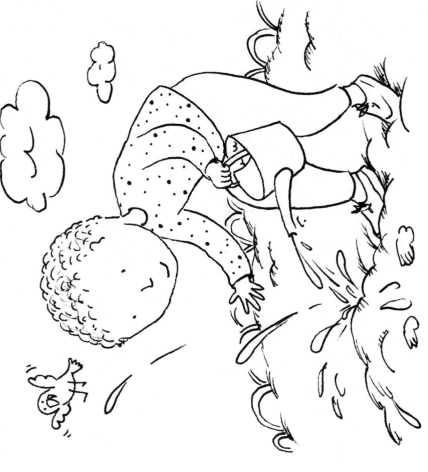

The earth feels dry.
It needs to be wet.
I water it a bit.
When will my seed grow?

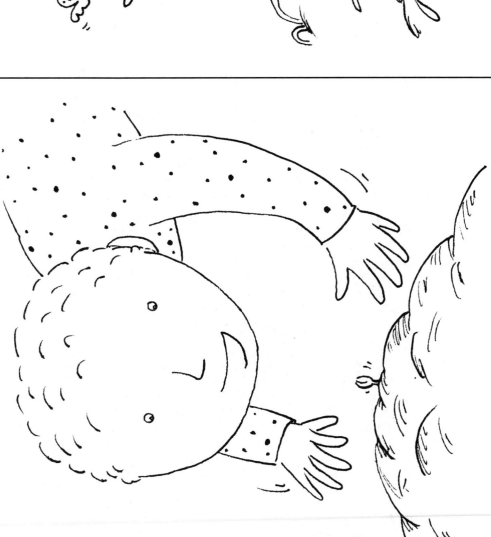

I look again.
I see something green!
It isn't very big.
Look at my seed grow!

⑤

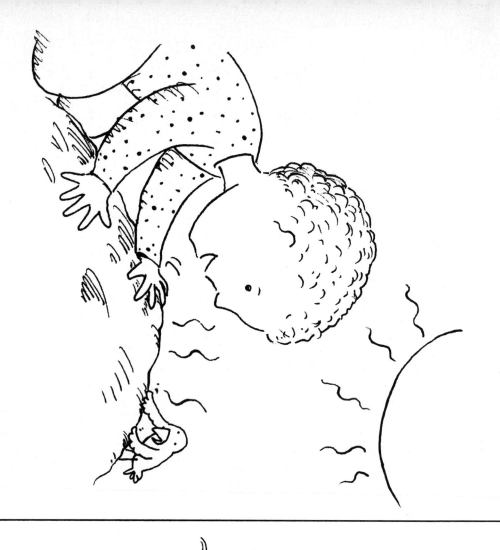

The sun comes out.
It warms up the earth.
My seed will warm up, too.
When will my seed grow?

③

I look each day.
I see nothing new.
The earth is only brown.
When will my seed grow?

④

# Helen Keller

Helen showed them how
to talk with their hands.
She helped them to read.
Helen Keller made life better
for many people.

⑦

Helen Keller lived long ago.
She was a happy baby.
Then Helen got sick.

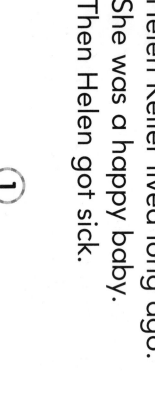

(1)

Helen began to help others.
She helped those who could not
see or hear.

(6)

Helen was not happy now.
She could not see.
She could not hear or talk.

②

Helen went to school.
She found out how
to make sounds.
She began to talk out loud!

⑤

Helen felt alone and sad.
Then a lady came to help.
Her name was Anne.
At first, Helen didn't want
Anne to help her.

③

Then Anne showed Helen
how to talk with her hands.
She helped Helen read
with her hands, too.

④

# Little Frog

Off came the mud and paint.
"I'm green again!" said Little Frog.
"Green is the color for me!"

7

Little Frog didn't like his color.
"I don't want to be green,"
he said.

1

Little Frog hopped away
from the bird. He hopped
into a pond.

6

Little Frog hopped into a can of paint. He hopped out again. The paint was red. Now Little Frog was red, too.

②

A bird saw Little Frog.
"A big worm!" sang the bird.
"I'll eat it!"
"I'm not a worm!" cried Little Frog.

⑤

Little Frog hopped down
the road. A cat saw him go by.
"A red bird!" said the cat.
"I'll eat it!"
"I'm not a bird!" cried Little Frog.

Little Frog hopped away
from the cat. He hopped
into a hole. It felt wet.
Little Frog hopped out.
He was brown with mud.

# How the Bear Lost Its Tail

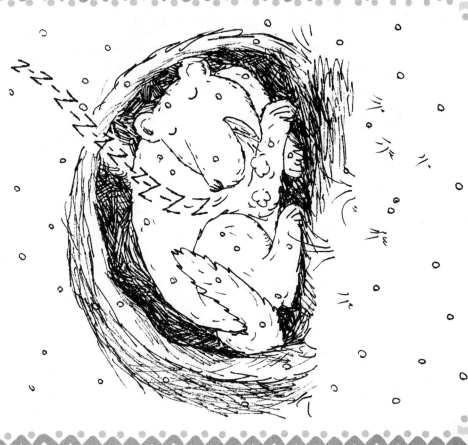

The bear raced after the fox. His long tail stayed in the ice. From that day on, the bear had no tail. That is why bears do not have tails today.

(7)

One cold day, a bear woke up.
He wanted food. The bear saw
a fox walk by.

1

The fox came by. He laughed.
"Did you catch any fish yet?"
he asked.
The bear cried out. He jumped
at the fox.

6